Raihanna's First Time Fasting

Written by Qamaer Hassan
Illustrated by Yasu M

Printed in the United States of America
First Printing, 2016
ISBN-13: 978-1530794652

ISBN-10: 153079465X

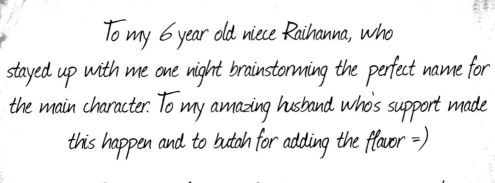

To my 6 year old niece Raihanna, who
stayed up with me one night brainstorming the perfect name for
the main character. To my amazing husband who's support made
this happen and to butah for adding the flavor =)

Stay tuned for more Raihanna stories to come!

–Qamaer Hassan

It was the night before Ramadan. Raihanna and her parents were decorating the living room.

They placed colorful lights along the living room walls, set lanterns on top of the fireplace, and finally, hung the big, bright, crescent-shaped moon and star in the center of their ceiling.

Their living room was shimmering just like the stars in the night sky.

Raihanna was super excited. She loved Ramadan, but this year's Ramadan was going to be extra special. This year, she decided that she was going to fast just like a big girl.

"Mama, how do we know when Ramadan begins?" she asked.

"Ramadan is the ninth month of the Islamic calendar, so to know the exact day, we follow the moon. When the moon is in a crescent shape, we know that it's Ramadan," replied her mom.

"What's a crescent?" asked Raihanna.

"It's a shape like a banana," her mom replied.

Raihanna and her Mom stepped out to the
porch. They both looked at the sky, waiting for the
crescent-shaped moon.

"I see it, Mama! The banana!" shouted Raihanna, as she pointed
towards the sky.

"You mean crescent," laughed Raihanna's mom. "And yes, you're right
and you know what that means."

"YAY! IT'S RAMADAN!" shouted Raihanna.

"It sure is. Now let's get you to bed because you're going to have to wake up extra early for *Suhoor*."

Raihanna was then tucked into bed by her dad.

Together, they read three verses from the Quran: *Surat Al-Falaq*, *Surat Al-Nas*, and *Surat Al-Ikhlas*.

"I'll wake you up in a few hours. Goodnight, habibti," said her dad as he kissed her forehead.

8

A few hours later, Raihanna was awakened to the smell of maple syrup pancakes and spiced *fasulya*, one of her favorite dishes.

She ran to the kitchen and began stuffing her mouth with chunks of beans and syrup.

"Raihanna, slow down. Are we in a race?" asked her father, laughing. "If so, you are totally winning."

"I want to make sure I eat all I can before *Salat Al-Fajr*, Baba; so I can be able to fast all day tomorrow just like you and Mama."

As soon as she finished eating, Raihanna put on her hijab so she can sit next to her parents in the living room while they waited for *Salat Al-Fajr*.

"Raihanna, did you know that the best time to make *Dua* is right before *Fajr*? Allah comes down to the lowest heaven and asks, who needs my help and forgiveness? Now, the special part of Ramadan is that Allah helps and forgives you even more," said Raihanna's mom.

"Allah will help me with anything … *anything*? And he'll forgive me for anything? Are you sure, mama?"

"Yes, if it's what's best for you. Allah loves to help, so all you have to do is ask."

So Raihanna raised her hands in front of her face, closed her eyes, and whispered,

"Oh Allah, forgive me for that time that I lied and told Mama I lost my cookie so that she would give me another one. And ... and forgive me for not sharing my toys with my cousin, Maryam; she never follows my rules and it gets me **MAD! OH!** And Allah, me and my best friend, Safiya, really want to go ice skating this week so if you can help make that happen that would be awesome! Ameen!"

That morning, Raihanna went to school with a big smile on her face. She was ready for her first day of fasting.

It all went well, until …

Snack time.

Ms. Collins didn't usually give out cookies for snack time, but today she did.

"No, thank you, Ms. Collins," replied Raihanna. "I'm fasting today."

Raihanna watched all the other kids eating their chunky, chocolate chip cookies.

"Raihanna, what's fasting?" asked Jennifer, one of her classmates.

"Is it like running really fast?" another classmate asked.

"It's when you don't eat all day," replied Raihanna.

"All day!" shouted both of her classmates in shock.

"That doesn't seem like fun," said Jennifer.

"Well, just until the sun goes down, then we can eat whatever we want," replied Raihanna.

"Why?" Jennifer asked.

Raihanna wasn't sure how to answer that question, so she just shrugged.

All she knew was that during Ramadan, all Muslims fast and that was what she wanted to do.

When Raihanna got home from school, her stomach started to growl. She missed having her peanut butter and jelly sandwich waiting for her.

"How is your first day of fasting going so far?" her mom asked.

"It's okay," mumbled Raihanna. "I'm just really hungry. How long until we eat?"

"A few more hours. Hang in there," said her Mom.

"UGGHHH." Raihanna placed her hand on her growling stomach.

"This is too hard. What's the point of fasting, anyway?"

GROWL

Raihanna's mom looked at her worried.

"I'm going out. Do you want to come along? It'll make the time pass."

"Ugh, fine," sighed Raihanna, as she dragged her feet out the door.

During the car ride, Raihanna kept asking:

"How many hours until we eat now?"

"And now?"

"How about now?"

"Is it time yet?"

"Only five minutes have passed, Raihanna," said her mom. "Be patient."

Soon enough, they stopped in front of a building. There was a really long line of men, women, and even children waiting outside.

"Where are we?" asked Raihanna.

"Come inside and I'll show you."

They walked into a dull grey room with tables and chairs, where people were eating.

There were people dressed in aprons and hairnets serving food.

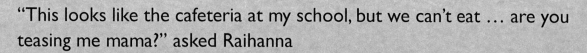

"This looks like the cafeteria at my school, but we can't eat … are you teasing me mama?" asked Raihanna

"Raihanna, these people are homeless. They have no food and no place to sleep, so this soup kitchen is a place to give them food and somewhere to stay for a little while.".

Raihanna was surprised to hear this. "Aren't they always hungry?"

"Yes, this is why we are here. It's our job as Muslims to help those in need. One of the most important parts of fasting is to understand how other people who don't have food feel, so that we can be thankful for our own blessings."

"What blessings do we have?"

"We have many blessings. Allah has showered us with the blessings of a home, a beautiful family, and Alhamdulillah, we always have something to eat. A lot of people in this world don't have that."

And that's when Raihanna realized there was more to fasting than just the hunger.

She felt guilty for complaining.

Raihanna gladly wore an apron, put on a hairnet, and helped her mom serve the food.

She made sure to smile at each and every person.

When they were finished, Raihanna looked up at her mom and asked,

"Mama, can we do this every day?"

"Of course, habibti," she replied as she held Raihanna in her arms.

When they finally arrived home, Raihanna was eager to help her dad set the table.

On the dining room table there were several dishes of rice and kofta, roasted chicken with vegetables, samboosa, bowls of soup, and lots and lots of dates — Raihanna's favorite.

Raihanna sat patiently at the table surrounded by the people she loved most.

To her right were her Khalu Malik, Khala Qamar, and Khalu Ismail; across from her were her Gidda and Khala Reem; and beside her sat Khala Layla and her cousin, Maryam.

As everybody grabbed a date and broke their fast, Raihanna suddenly felt sorry for all the people she met today who didn't have any food, or family to be with.

So Raihanna closed her eyes, raised up both her hands in front of her face, and started to make Dua.

"Oh Allah, please help all the poor people and give them food to eat. I also want to thank you for blessing me with my family and home, so you can forget the ice skating. Ameen."

This was how Raihanna spent the next twenty-nine days of Ramadan and she loved every second of it!

Raihanna wishes you and your family a blessed Ramadan just like hers.

Definition

Suhoor - is an Islamic term referring to the meal consumed early in the morning by Muslims before fasting, in daylight hours during the Islamic month of Ramadan.

Surat Al Falaq – (The Dawn) Verse in the holy Quran

Surat Al-Nas – (The Mankind) Verse in the holy Quran

Surat Al- Ikhlas – (Purity) Verse in the holy Quran

Fasulya - Smashed up beans in spices

Allah - God

Salat Al-Fajr – Prayer before sunrise

Alhamdulillah – Thank god

Kofta – Rolled up meat

Samboosa - Spring rolls stuffed with beef

Khala's - Aunts

Khalu - Uncle

Gidda - Grandmother

Athan – Call for prayer

Dua – Supplication

Ameen - Amen

I am thankful to Allah for blessing me with...

1. _____   5. _____

2. _____   6. _____

3. _____   7. _____

4. _____   8. _____

My Dua List

_____

_____

_____

_____

_____

_____

Made in the USA
Middletown, DE
06 June 2016